The A-Z of Amazon.co.uk FBA

A step-by-step guide to branding, sourcing and selling private-label FBA products on Amazon's UK website

ISBN: 9781522061977

2020 edition

Ned Browne

About the author

Ned Browne spent his early career working for some of London's best-known advertising agencies including Saatchi & Saatchi, TBWA and Collett Dickenson Pearce, helping create award-winning campaigns and developing strengths in marketing, branding and digital. Latterly, he has worked in journalism, property development/consultancy, brand and product development, online marketing and education.

Ned Browne is also the Reader's Digest's long-term property correspondent. He has advised numerous would-be property owners, helping many get onto the property ladder.

By the same author:

How to get onto the property ladder *- A first-time buyer's guide to financing and finding your first home*

Love University *- How to survive and thrive at university*

Content

Introduction

There are countless FBA books, but none that focus on Amazon's UK website. This book aims to fill that gap. I didn't plan to write a book, rather a guide for my own use – to make the process easier. However, when various friends and family members asked for copies, I set about writing a full-length book that could be made available to the wider community.

My other issues with current FBA books is that they invariably make claims such as, "How I made $90,000 in 90 days" etc. This may or may not be true. But I wouldn't advise quitting your day job. Start small, enjoy the process and hopefully in time you'll reap the rewards.

What is FBA?

FBA stands for Fulfilled By Amazon - in other words, Amazon stores and ships products on your behalf. They take a cut and you get access to their customers and Prime delivery.

Amazon rarely publishes its Prime membership number by country, but independent research has suggested that there are over 15 million members in the UK alone. That would make sense, as Amazon recently reported that there were 150 million Prime members worldwide. And Prime members spend more - over double what non-Prime customers spend. This wrap-around service has proved very popular and extremely sticky – renewal rates are close to 100%. At just £79 a year (or £7.99 a month) for next day delivery it's a compelling offer. Plus it's recruiting customers young: Amazon Prime Student costs just £39 a year.

Amazon Prime offers its UK customers a huge range of benefits, including:
- Unlimited one-day (and in some areas same-day) delivery on millions of items.
- Prime Video - unlimited video streaming of thousands of TV shows and movies.

- Unlimited photo storage on Prime Photos.
- Access to the Kindle Lending Library where customers can choose from over 600,000 titles.
- Access to 'Prime Day' shopping discounts.

No wonder almost every Prime member renews each year.

In research conducted by Amazon.co.uk, 85% of sellers who had switched to FBA reported a sales increase, and 53% reported a sales uplift of over 20% or more. Selling via FBA also gives you access to the Buy Box – i.e. you become the automatic seller if the customer clicks on the main "Add to Basket" button. This is vital if you're one of a number of sellers selling the same product.

FBA allows you to spend your time on what's important: product design, branding and finance. You don't have to worry about being hacked or setting up payment systems. There's no more traipsing to the Post Office or worrying about being away when an order needs to be fulfilled. This gives you freedom too – you can run your FBA operation from anywhere in the world. All you need is access to the Internet.

Also, thanks to the introduction of pan-European FBA, sellers can sell their goods online in Europe. Amazon has unified its European marketplaces, meaning sellers can have access to several marketplaces, including Amazon.co.uk, Amazon.fr, Amazon.de, Amazon.it and Amazon.es. Of course, this may all change when the post-Brexit transition period ends on 31/12/2020. Watch this space.

But there are downsides too – Amazon has strict rules and procedures to follow. If you don't adhere to these, your products could be refused or delisted.

Why sell online and on Amazon?

According to recent research, online shopping spend in the UK is set to grow by 30% by 2024. And Amazon is likely to take the largest chunk of this growth: Amazon's sales growth has far outstripped that forecast over the last decade, having grown by 20%+ annually during that period. Global e-commerce consultancy eMarketer reckons 38% of all money spent online goes to Amazon.

Amazon are also perfectly positioned to take advantage of the growth in voice ordering - they have sold over 100 million Alexa-enabled devices. Moreover, if the "internet of things" does, in fact, become a thing, Amazon will be at the forefront. To the uninitiated, the theory of the internet of things is that everyday objects (such as fridges) will become smart - thus enabling them to send and receive data. So your fridge, for example, will know what to order from Amazon - and it will make that order seamlessly in the background.

Plus, over 50% of Amazon's sales are made via third-party sellers. And many of these are now FBAers.

Furthermore, UK consumers are the European kings of online shopping. Per capita, UK consumers outspend every other European country hands down. We spend 50% more per capita than our German neighbours (and they are the third most prolific online shoppers in Europe).

Amazon.co.uk has also been crowned the best British company for customer service by the Institute of Customer Service more than once, beating the likes of John Lewis and First Direct. Its range of products, compelling prices and unrivalled logistics operation means they're likely to get an increasingly large slice of the pie. And, as a FBA seller, you get to trade off Amazon's reputation.

Amazon customers are willing to pay higher prices for new products compared to eBay customers. That means you can charge more for your products. There are numerous reasons for this:

- The quality of the listings – eBay still looks a bit like a car-boot sale. eBay is where customers search for one-off oddities. But, if they want new, quality products they'll head to Amazon.
- Amazon's rating system is mainly product focused – Excellent customer service is a given.

- Amazon also protects customers with their A to Z Guarantee. It's easy to return products and to get refunds.
- Amazon customers can easily make changes to orders prior to shipment and can track orders online.
- Gift-wrap – Amazon will gift-wrap products for customers. That includes your FBA products.
- It's easier to shop on Amazon – Each individual product has just one listing (even if there are numerous sellers).
- Buy now with 1-Click – This feature allows customers to complete their purchase with, literally, a touch of a button. It's a particularly good feature on Amazon's mobile app.
- Mobile friendly – Amazon's mobile app burns eBay's. This is important as over 50% of e-commerce is now m-commerce (mobile-commerce) - and almost 90% of UK adults now own smartphones.
- Prime – Of course. Prime customers love Prime. 'Nuff said.

To join the party, the first thing you need to decide is what to sell.

Creating your product shortlist

This book will take you through all the steps to get your product made, branded and sold. However, it's up to you to decide on your first product. It's not a purely formulaic process, but there are some things that will help you decide which product to choose:

- Make sure it weighs less than two pounds – This will save on postage costs.
- Fix the selling price between £8 and £40 – This will allow you to make a reasonable amount of profit on each sale and many of Amazon's bestsellers fall into this price bracket.
- Consider "repeat purchase" products – Many household goods are bought time and time again.
- Stick to hard-to-break items – It's not uncommon for products to get broken in transit. For your initial product, choose something that's unlikely to break.

- Look at the competition – You can search for bestselling products, most gifted and most wished for on Amazon. Google, "best selling <<insert product>> on Amazon.co.uk" or search on Amazon's website. It's also worth looking at what's selling well on other websites, such as AliExpress.
- Reviews are important too – if you can find a product where there are high sales but no single product is universally praised, this is a niche worth investigating further. Many people rely on reviews to aid their decision-making process.
- While you're looking at customer reviews, spend time reading the negative ones. Sometimes a product just needs to be tweaked to make it infinitely better.
- Can you make a profit? – This will be covered in more detail later in the book. However, as a rule of thumb, you need to be able to sell the product for four times (or more) the initial purchase price. There are lots of costs to take into account such as VAT, import duty, shipping etc.
- Identify where there are only unbranded goods currently being sold – Before Havaianas took off in the 1990s there were no branded flip-flops. What generic products are out there that you could brand? Note: people buy products for rational reasons, but they buy brands for emotional reasons (or to keep up with the Joneses). That's why branded goods sell for far more.
- Identify where there is no premium product – There are lots of people with far too much money. They want premium everything – toilet brushes, butter dishes etc.
- Have a Unique Selling Proposition (USP) – If your product is different, you have a better chance of standing out. A product can differ in many different ways: brand, features, packaging, design etc.
- Be aware of the product life cycle – Some non-perishable, usually high-tech, products may have a short sales window, say 18 months. Initially, it's probably worth focusing on products that won't date too fast.

- Look at products that are Internet-friendly – Certain items are hard to find on the high street. For example, left-handed scissors.

Top tip: If you're struggling for ideas, check out Jungle Scout, who claim they will show "you the exact products that will make you money". For more details, follow this link: https://www.junglescout.com/uk/

Other ideas to help you decide what to sell

Someone once said, "Do a job you love and you'll never go to work again." That's true with FBA too – choose products that you would buy yourself or ones that you feel passionate about. That way it will keep your interest and you'll be far more likely to understand your customers. A friend of mine is a yoga nut – he sells yoga equipment online. Makes sense.

Problems are a great source of ideas. If you can't find durable gardening gloves, the chances are that you're not alone. Make a list of these and ask your friends too.

Flick through newspapers and magazines – they are awash with product ideas. And, if you can bear it, shopping channels will give you an insight into the kind of things people are buying. Pinterest is great for inspiration too.

You can also find out what customers are searching for on Amazon's website by typing in the start of a search. When I typed "pillow", the following appeared: pillows, pillow cases, emoji pillow, travel pillow, pregnancy pillow etc.

Product bundling is worth considering too. It's a tried and tested technique across a range of industries and used by everyone from car manufacturers (Ford + insurance) to the fast-food industry (McDonald's Happy Meal) and from games consoles (PlayStation + free game) to fine foods (Fortnum & Mason's hampers). The key advantage is that you can create a unique listing using off-the-shelf products. And you can charge less per item. For example, you could fill a wash-bag with toiletries, rebrand, barcode etc. and suddenly you have a unique offering. The reason you can charge a lower price is simple: Amazon's fees are less as they're only selling and shipping one item. It's also harder for competitors to copy your inventory.

Note: There are some Amazon rules regarding bundling. For example, BMVD (Books, Music, Videos, and DVDs) product bundles must be defined by the publisher or manufacturer and have a single ISBN, UPC or EAN.

Selling multipacks also allows you to sell your products at a lower per-unit price too. But, remember, if you're selling generic products this offering can be copied.

I urge you to avoid selling low-cost inventory. It's almost impossible to sell anything for less than £4 and make a profit, even if you can source it for pennies. The cost to ship to Amazon's fulfilment centre and Amazon's fees will decimate your profit.

Some new sellers piggyback existing listings. This is reasonable to test the market, but there are some significant downsides. Firstly you will not, initially at least, "own" the Buy box – you will be listed under "Other Sellers on Amazon". (Note: In Amazon's words, the "eligibility to win the Buy Box is tied to specific seller performance criteria that identify the sellers who have consistently provided customers with a great buying experience".) In addition, you're stuck with the listing they created, which may have poor pictures, a substandard description and be underpinned with irrelevant search terms.

This is one such example for a pretty generic sunglasses case: there were 17 sellers of the same item. The non-Prime price ranged from £1.33 to £1.70 including P&P. All these sellers were based in Hong Kong. It was also available on Prime for £4.32. So, unless you're in a rush, you're not going to buy from the Prime seller.

My first ever products were cushion covers. They did, in time, become the highest rated cushion covers on Amazon.co.uk. However, I made several mistakes:

- It was already a very competitive segment (which was price competitive too).
- I didn't get my logo stitched onto the covers.
- I didn't get an exclusivity deal on the designs.

Over time, I rectified these issues – but I wish I had known then what I know now.

The importance of branding

Many online FBA "gurus" advocate "flipping" products on Amazon. In other words, buy in bulk from wholesalers or manufacturers and sell for a profit on Amazon. But here's the rub: anyone can copy you. Worse still, people with bigger buying power can negotiate a lower cost-per-unit price, and are thus able to undercut your price. Furthermore, if you end up with a bestseller and that product is available "off the shelf", Amazon will start selling it. After all, they know what's selling well and they will always win the price war.

Unbranded products also sell for less. I know, no one knows your brand. It's brand new (excuse the pun). But that doesn't really matter. Research has shown that people will pay up to a third more – even when they have never heard of the brand. It's amazing what a brand name and a cool logo can do. And creating a brand is much easier than you think. Philip Knight, who founded Nike, famously paid Carolyn Davidson just $35 to design their now-famous Swoosh logo. And, thanks to the Internet, it's much easier now.

Branding is especially important if you're thinking about an "exit strategy". Unbranded products are easy to copy, so what's your company worth? I would suggest not very much. Creating a brand will give you far more options down the line, including the ability to sell your products through offline channels. And, of course, it will make your company more valuable if you ever come to sell your business.

In very simple terms, a brand is a name and a logo. That's the start point anyway. Down the line, it will become associated with your products, your advertising and your company values. But, to start with, you need a name.

Spend time getting this right now. Ignore those who suggest this can be fixed later. Maybe so, but potentially at a high cost – for example, reprinting labels, redesigning websites etc. In terms of starting, think about the kind of products you're selling. My friend selling yoga equipment chose the name "adho" (a yoga pose).

As your brand name gathers traction, it helps with searches too. Having a unique name allows potential customers to find your products on Amazon.

Produce a shortlist of names and then invite friends to a focus group (disguised as a dinner party) to discuss your ideas. The shortlist should also be informed by domain name availability. I've always found www.123-reg.co.uk an excellent website for this task. It allows backorders too – so should a domain become available it will automatically purchase it on your behalf.

Once you have decided upon your brand name, you'll need to get a logo. Check out https://uk.fiverr.com/ if you need a designer. The advantage of such websites is that they link you to talented people from all over the world. It also allows you to see loads of examples of their work and pay developing/emerging market prices. It's probably worth getting a number of designs and researching these too. But don't over-research – sometimes you need to back your hunch. In the words of Henry Ford, "If I had asked people what they wanted, they would have said faster horses."

Top tip: You may need a simplified version of your logo for reproduction purposes.

Registering a trademark

If you are serious about building a brand, you should register your trademark. A registered trademark is usually a combination of your company name and logo.

The main advantage of having a registered trademark is that no one can then use your brand without your permission. It also allows you to put the ® symbol next to your logo. And, in the future, you may even be able to sell or license your brand.

You need to register your trademark within the category with which it's most closely associated. If you envisage entering associated markets, it's worth including them too. Although, the more categories the greater the cost.

The registration process takes about fours months, assuming that no one objects. Registered trademarks then last 10 years, but the renewal process is little more than a formality.

To register your trademark, click on this link:
https://www.gov.uk/how-to-register-a-trade-mark

Note: Registering your trademark in the UK only protects your brand in the UK.

Top tip: It's worth checking already-registered trademarks before you decide on your final brand. After all, you don't want a third party to use their trademark registration to try to prevent you selling and marketing your products further down the line.

Importing goods

Note: This may all change on the 1st January 2021. How things will change, no one knows. It all depends on the EU/UK Brexit trade negotiations. But, for the time being, this is what you need to know:

All importers need an EORI number to clear customs. EORI stands for Economic Operator Registration and Identification. When you're applying for your VAT number you can apply for your EORI at the same time. (If you already have a VAT number (VRN), your EORI number will be GB + Your VRN + 000 (e.g. GB012345678000).)

For importers who choose not to be VAT registered, you can still get an EORI number: www.gov.uk/guidance/eori-supporting-guidance

If you need to register for VAT, Google "registering for VAT" or go to: https://online.hmrc.gov.uk/registration/newbusiness/business-allowed

You also need to ascertain your product's Commodity Code. Commodity Codes are used to establish your import duty. The rate can range widely depending on what you're importing. So, do your research before placing your order.

All Commodity Codes are listed here: www.gov.uk/trade-tariff/a-z-index/a?country=&day=2&month=9&year=2015

If you're still unsure, ask the manufacturer and they should be able to provide you with the correct code.

Sourcing products

It's hard to beat Alibaba when sourcing products. Alibaba are a Chinese e-commerce juggernaut – they're effectively a wholesaler, Amazon and eBay all rolled into one. In China, its Tmall platform is modeled on Amazon, and its Taobao platform is an eBay clone. (Oh, and it also owns or has stakes in Juhuasuan (a Chinese version of Groupon), Alipay.com

(Paypal), Sina Weibo (Twitter) and Youku Tudou (YouTube)). Founded in 1999, it handles over 50% of China's e-commerce and has over 550 million active users.

Alibaba is also where buyers in the West can find suppliers (wholesalers and manufacturers) in the Far East. More than eight million suppliers sell on Alibaba and there's an almost endless list of products you can buy.

But there are pitfalls too. Remember, you may technically be the client, but most suppliers want to be reassured you're not a fly-by-night operator and are likely to place future and larger orders. Your first email of introduction is crucial.

Here's an example:

Dear sir/madam

I am the owner of a company based in the United Kingdom.

We're currently looking for reliable suppliers with which to do long-term business.

Having researched numerous products, we have been particularly impressed with your genuine leather handbags.

Are you able to produce bespoke versions to our exacting needs? For example:
- Different colours.
- Adding our brand.
- Different catch.
- Etc.

If so, I will provide exact specifications upon receipt of your email.

Also, just so we know, how much would 1,000 units of your current design cost (FOB price)?

I look forward to hearing from you. Thank you in advance for your help.

All the best

Ned Browne

In this piece of communication, I have:
- Stated that I want to become a long-term business partner.
- Paid them a compliment.
- Asked about customising.
- Reaffirmed I'm serious by suggesting a 1,000 order.
- Been polite.

Note: FOB = Free On Board (i.e. once they've shipped the product, it's your responsibility to pay the VAT and import duty).

I tend to say I'm the owner. However, others advocate claiming to be the "Purchasing Manager" to make the company sound bigger.

The trick is to start a conversation. Once they have replied to your initial email, it's far easier to keep things going with timely replies of your own.

If I have a new product in mind, I tend to send my initial enquiry to 10-15 possible suppliers. This will help you choose the right one.

How to choose a supplier on Alibaba

This isn't an exact science, but you can certainly increase your odds of succeeding. The first thing to consider is the different levels of Alibaba verification. Not all companies are what they seem - fake companies, replete with photos of factories and employees, spring up online on a weekly basis. It's pretty easy to set up as an Alibaba seller, and Alibaba only undertakes rudimentary checks on most of its sellers. Here are the three levels of verification:

- "A&V Checked suppliers are Gold Suppliers who have passed authentication and verification inspection by Alibaba.com as well as a third-party verification company. All legal business licenses and contact persons are verified for those who have been A&V Checked." This all sounds very reassuring. But, in fact, Alibaba has only checked their business license and contact information.

- "Onsite Check is a verification process for China Gold Suppliers. The supplier's company's premises are checked by Alibaba.com's staff to ensure onsite operations exist there. The suppliers' legal status and other related information are then confirmed by a third-party verification agency." For these suppliers, Alibaba has also made a number of additional checks, including the company/factory location, the ownership status of the premises and photos of the supplier's operations. So, this is a step up.

- "Assessed Supplier is an Alibaba.com service providing you with fully independent and impartial third-party verification of your prospective suppliers. We commission several agencies based on their international reputation and proven credibility to test the claims made by suppliers. For buyers, this means that instinct and trust are based only on concrete evidence. Assessed Supplier includes Assessment Reports Verified Videos and Verified Main Products." In fairness to Alibaba, these suppliers do seem to be fully vetted.

For more information, click on this link:
https://service.alibaba.com/buyer/ab/safety_security/products/verificati on_services.php

Pay careful attention to their existing products. If you don't see anything you like, move on fast. If you like their product range (or certain items within it), consider the following: How much would they have to change to meet your needs? Do they seem to be of a high standard?

You should also take note of their MOQ (Minimum Order Quantity). Some seem to have ridiculously high minimum-order requirements. Don't let that completely put you off – if they seem like a good supplier in every other regard, contact them too. They can only say "no" (or not reply to your enquiry).

Some people also look for ISO-accredited suppliers. ISO (the International Organization for Standardization) is an independent body that helps facilitate world trade by providing common standards between nations. Companies that follow these standards should, in theory, manufacture products that are safe, reliable and of good quality. The standards also serve to safeguard your customers.

Check out their response rate too – don't waste your time emailing anyone scoring less than 50%. On that subject, how long have they been trading for? Less than two years would make me nervous.

You should now have a long shortlist. This is to whom you send your initial 10-15 emails, the responses to which will help you whittle down your list further:

- Did they respond in a timely manner?
- Did they supply the information you requested?
- How was their written English? Remember: you may have to supply detailed and complex manufacturing requirements. Are you confident these won't be lost in translation?

At this point I've found that about 60% of suppliers tend not to hit the mark, which should leave you with half a dozen or fewer, thus creating your short shortlist. These are the companies from whom you should request a quote. Below is an example of a quote-request email:

Dear Natalie

Thank you for your email. I hope we can work together. As promised, this email should provide you with all the details you need.

Here are the belt production specifications:

- Solid brass roller buckle (approx. 2 inches X 2 inches) – see "Brass buckle.jpg" (attached).
- The belt should be 1.5 inches wide. Full grain vegetable tanned leather (cowhide) approx. 4 mm thick that will develop a patina with age.
  - It has to smell of leather.
- Belt loop – 0.5 inches wide. Made from 6mm leather. Stitched and glued into place.
- Four brass rivets to hold the "return" in place – two each side of the belt loop.
- Seven holes.
- Colour – as close to the "Colour reference.jpg" (attached) belt colour as possible.
- Three things would need to be stamped onto the inside of the belt:
  - Genuine leather (see attached example).
  - The size – S, M, L, XL.
  - Our company logo (simplified version)

I require four sizes – please see attached JPEGs for exact dimensions.

Is it possible to make a sample belt initially? I am happy to pay for this. Just let me know the price.

Also, based on this specification, could you please provide a FOB price for 150 of each size (i.e. 600 belts in total)? Assuming these belts sell well, I will order larger quantities later this year.

Thank you in advance for your help.

In this piece of communication, I have:

- Referred to the person who initially replied by name.
- Given as much detail as possible.
- Provided design diagrams.

- Provided several reference images.
- Again I have referred to the fact that I am hoping to order in larger quantities at a later date.

This email was sent to five suppliers, of whom four provided a quote within 24 hours. The FOB price varied from approximately £5 to £8 per unit. The company I eventually chose didn't provide the cheapest quote, but the quality of their communication far surpassed their rivals. And, based on the lower quotes, I was able to negotiate the price down to £5 and get the sample cost refunded. Lesson learned: getting multiple quotes and negotiating are key.

One thing that I didn't do, but might be worth considering, is getting a range of prices for different quantities. This is a great way to determine when viable economies of scale kick in. It may be at the 100-unit level, 200-unit level or 10,000-unit level. Knowing this helps you determine how many units you should order.

Top tip: Certain products (e.g. toys) require a CE mark to be sold within the EU. The letters "CE" are the abbreviation of the French phrase "Conformité Européene", which literally means "European Conformity". For a full list, see the "Rules and Regulations" chapter. If your product is on that list, check with your supplier that it will comply with EU safety rules and can be CE marked.

Another factor affecting my choice of supplier is their ability to offer a holistic service. Typically, I expect the supplier to:
- Manufacture the product.
- Check product quality.
- Add branding and other labels.
- Print and add a review request card.
- Print barcodes and attach to each product.
- Print Amazon's delivery labels and attach to each carton.
- Ensure the products comply with EU safety rules and are, if necessary, CE marked.
- Arrange shipment.

- Provide detailed product information, including dimensions, materials, weight etc.
- Source suitable packaging (and add branding if necessary).

It's worth spending time on the latter as packaging serves a dual purpose: preventing your product being damaged/preventing injuries (See "FBA Packaging Restrictions" in the "Rules and Regulations" chapter) and creating a good first impression. I sometimes wonder if the key difference between products bought on eBay and Amazon is the quality of the packaging. The packaging branding could simply take the form of your logo stuck onto the outside. If volumes increase, you may decide to get it pre-printed onto the packaging.

Note: Amazon will over-pack your products with Amazon-branded packaging – your product could be delivered in a larger box alongside several other items. The average order spend on Amazon is in the region of £35 – Prime customers are likely to spend more per order.

Top tip: Most people source their products on Alibaba, but it's also worth checking out other websites such as www.hktdc.com

Buying on Alibaba

Once you are confident the supplier has been briefed perfectly, you should order a pre-production sample. (Some suppliers will refund this cost when you place a bulk order.) Expect to pay approximately double your final selling price for this one-off. This may seem expensive, but it's not nearly as expensive as ending up with unsellable stock.

Assuming you're happy with the sample, you can place your order. But how many to order? This is a difficult question to answer as it depends on many factors, including:
- Your cash flow.
- Your attitude to risk.
- Your experience.

However, it's fair to say that most people test new products on a relatively small scale initially – say 100 units. That's high enough to keep the stock purchase price reasonably low and enough to get a reasonable number of customer reviews (and traction) on Amazon. Remember, if you can make a profit on your initial order, you're almost guaranteed to make more when you reorder in larger quantities.

Top tip: Q4 sales (i.e. October, November and December) are typically 40% higher compared to Q3. Christmas and Black Friday are massive for Amazon – don't get stitched up by running out of stock.

How to pay for your goods

There are various methods for paying for your goods. Here are the main ones:
- Escrow – This is definitely a very reasonable option. A third party holds your money until you confirm the satisfactory delivery of your order. As such, Escrow protects both parties.
- PayPal – This is my payment method of choice. It's definitely buyer friendly, easy to use and comes with fairly good buyer protection. However, sellers are not so keen, as PayPal tends to favour buyers when disputes arise.
- Upfront Telegraphic Transfer (TT) Bank Transfer – The buyer receives all the money before production begins. As a buyer this can leave you exposed, as there's little recourse if things go wrong. However, if you have used a supplier before and trust them, it's an efficient method of payment. Note: your bank will almost certainly charge you for making an international transfer. Mine charge me £25. Robbers!
- TransferWise app. Some suppliers will insist on a bank transfer. If so, TransferWise will almost certainly be cheaper than your bank. They are definitely cheaper than mine.

But before you place your order you need to list your product on Amazon.

Registering as a seller on Amazon

You need the following things to complete the registration:
· Credit card.
· Phone number.
· Company registration details (if relevant).
· Primary contact person information.
· Beneficial owner information.
· Bank account information.

Google "setting up a seller account on Amazon.co.uk" and click on the top link – it will take you to the correct Amazon page. The registration process is pretty straightforward.

Seller Central

When you log in as a seller, your home page is Seller Central – this is the hub of your operation and there's a wealth of information at your fingertips. To get there, click on "Your Account" and then "Sell on Amazon" (sign in using your standard Amazon log-in details). Take some time to explore this Aladdin's Cave. In particular, scroll over the various tabs (such as Inventory, Pricing, Orders, Advertising, Reports and Performance) along the top. Click on any of the links that take your interest. As your experience grows, you'll find new things of note every day.

Seller Central is surprisingly user friendly. Don't be overwhelmed by the volume of content; it's designed with every type of seller in mind. Not everything will be relevant – but finding what is tends to be pretty straightforward. On the odd occasion I've struggled, a quick Google search has swiftly brought me to the correct Amazon page. I've also found YouTube an invaluable resource. Although there's a huge US bias, there are thousands of "how to" videos, some of which are excellent. If you're still stuck, you can click on the "Get support" button on the bottom left of your Seller Central page – this will allow you to email Amazon your query.

Seller Central vs. Vendor Central

If you sell via Seller Central – yes, that's all of you – Amazon considers you to be a marketplace or third-party seller. Amazon Vendor Central is the web interface used by manufacturers and distributors. If you sell via Vendor Central, you're considered a first-party seller. You're acting as a supplier, selling in bulk to Amazon. It's not a party that's easily gatecrashed – it's invitation only.

Listing FBA products on Amazon

The first thing you need is a barcode. These can be bought off-the-shelf from a number of different online suppliers. I use www.buyabarcode.co.uk - but that's mainly force of habit. You can get them cheaper here:
www.barcodesmania.co.uk

Top tip: Barcodes will come with two numbers: EAN = Europe only. UPC = worldwide. On Amazon.co.uk you should use the EAN number.

However, you should be aware that, strictly speaking, you are buying a generic barcode. Although it will be unique, it will not identify the country of origin, the manufacturer/supplier or the specific product (nor will it have a "check digit"). This is why EAN codes were initially set up: to help identify this information.

If you scale up, you should probably obtain your barcodes from GS1 www.gs1uk.org/. They are expensive though - the initial joining fee alone is £130.80+.

FBA Labeled Inventory vs. Stickerless, Commingled Inventory

As an FBA seller, you'll be asked to choose "FBA Labeled Inventory" (default setting) or "Stickerless, Commingled Inventory". Here's how they differ:

- FBA Labeled Inventory - You print your product labels from Seller Central, which must be applied to each unit you ship to Amazon's fulfilment centres.
- Stickerless, Commingled Inventory - Your products don't require FBA labels, as they are treated as identical to units of the same product from other sellers (who have also selected Stickerless, Commingled Inventory). When a customer orders one of these products from you, you are the seller of record – i.e. you get the money for the sale. But the product used to fulfill the order may have been sourced from either another seller's or Amazon's own inventory.

I only sell products that are unique (in terms of branding, design, USP or all three), so I use FBA Labeled Inventory.

The second thing you need is a brand name. Once you have these two you are ready to list your own unique products on Amazon.

To do this:
- Go to "Your Seller Account".
- Scroll over "Inventory" and select "Manage Inventory".

At this point, you need to select a product category. If you're not sure where to locate your item, Google "best selling <<insert product name>> on Amazon.co.uk". Once you've clicked on the product, scroll down to "Product details" and next to the "Amazon Bestsellers Rank" you'll see the categories and subcategories. Use these to put your product into the correct category. Note: If the exact categories don't match up, you're not doing anything wrong – sometimes they don't.

Top tip: If you're changing from seller fulfilled to FBA, you can do this by selecting "Inventory" and then "Manage Inventory". Tick relevant product (on the left hand side) and then select "Convert to Fulfilled by Amazon" from the "Action on << >> Selected".

The first section you need to complete is "Vital info". This is where you add your item title, brand name and barcode number. (More information can be added later.) The barcode number is crucial. If this is not correctly entered, everything else falls apart. The EAN enables Amazon to identify the products in their giant fulfilment centres. When you've entered this information, click on "Save and finish".

Once you have saved this initial information, Amazon will create an ASIN (Amazon Standard Identification Number) and a SKU (Stock Keeping Number).

When creating your product-heading, make sure you include the brand name, name of product, keywords and your Unique Selling Proposition (if you have one). In terms of Search Engine Optimization (SEO), longer is better. You may also want to consider such things as: premium, retro, vintage, modern, material, colour, size etc.

But beware of gaining more views at the expense of sales. For example, if you're selling black handbags, and you include a range of colours in your title (for example, handbag - red / blue / yellow / pink / black) you will get more views but almost certainly fewer sales.

Your photos are very important. The Internet is not the perfect platform to showcase products, so imagery is vital. Here's a summary of Amazon's product image guidelines:
- Products must fill at least 85% of the image.
- Main images must have a pure white background, must be a photo and must not contain excluded accessories.
- Images must be at least 1,000 pixels on the longest side and at least 500 pixels on the shortest side.
- JPEG is the preferred image format.

These have been put in place to prevent Amazon looking like eBay. If you don't follow the rules your listing could be taken down. And, even if that doesn't happen, your sales will suffer if you have poor quality pictures.

Amazon allows up to nine images – you should have at least six. Both high resolution and multiple images have been shown to improve conversion rates. Photograph your product from different angles and consider adding your company logo as the final image.

Getting the white background is something else you can outsource to Fiverr. The person I use is based in Vietnam who charges £3.50 for ten images. Alternatively, there are now background removing apps - Magic Eraser is particularly good.

Top tip: Amazon encourages sellers to upload images larger than 1000 x 1000 pixels, the size required to activate their zoom feature, and says, "Zoom has proven to enhance sales."

Product description/bullet points

This is another case of more is better. Make sure you write a long description – 200 words is a reasonable starting point. Describe the product in detail. Tell your/your company story too. And make sure customers know you're a UK business.

But, perhaps, your five bullet points are more important. They feature next to the image. Most sellers are convinced that buyers spend more time looking at bullet points (as opposed to the product description). So, you have to nail them.

You're allowed five bullet points for each listing. Each bullet point is limited to 500 characters. Your bullet points should give your potential customers all the information they need – if they have to scroll down to the product description, you haven't done your job. The description should be the cherry on the cake.

Top tips for creating bullet points:
- The first bullet point should highlight the most relevant feature/benefit. You should then work your way down the list - the fifth bullet point being your least relevant feature/benefit.

- Use your research (primary and secondary) to find out what's most important to your customers. Look at your competitors' product reviews for more ideas.
- Give prominence to your Unique Selling Proposition.
- Has your main competitor's product got an Achilles' heel? If so, you may want to include a bullet point starting with, "Unlike…".
- Make them interesting:
  - Boring: "100% leather".
  - Marginally better: "100% Italian vegetable-tanned leather".
  - The daddy: "100% Italian vegetable-tanned aged leather (cowhide). It smells great too – imagine the leather seats in a vintage Rolls Royce."
- Consider encouraging an action – For example, "Roll over the images to see the quality", or "Please read the reviews from our customers".
- Some other things to consider including:
  - Materials (e.g. stainless steel).
  - Size, dimensions and weight.
  - Special care instructions (e.g. hand wash only).
  - Where the product was made (especially if it was made in the UK or somewhere famous for making that product. For example, Swiss watches).
  - Warranty and guarantee information.
- Review and amend your product's bullet points down the line, in light of customer feedback or questions posed by customers.

Here's a lovely example from Amazon.co.uk (product description and bullet points):

Urban Safari London – Lincoln Satchel
The best things in life get better with age. Our bags are no exception. Made from genuine goat hide leather, hand-stitched for durability, and aged using only natural oils, our bags are built to last - with looks that just keep on improving over the years.

Delivering classic vintage styling, these satchels are the perfect shoulder bag for everyday use - whether it's work, college or travel. Strong and lightweight too, they're great for books, folders, photography gear, in fact anything. And, at 16 inches makes the perfect bag for any laptop (we've also added in a padded central interior section to keep your machine even safer).

What makes Urban Safari different?

We believe in creating a quality satchel that lasts and ensure best possible practices from start to finish - hides are individually all handpicked for quality, not bought in bulk. We then wash them seven times, only then are they tanned professionally. We can assure you, unlike our competitors, our bags will only ever smell beautifully of real leather.

We only use quality components. All of our bags utilise heavy-duty burnished brass buckles, rivets and zips. Not only does this mean they last a lifetime, they also look much better and compliment the natural colour of the leather. For the interior we use strong khaki canvas lining (see our photos), with padded sections for your laptop.

- Timeless classic satchel with front pocket detail in stunning aged real leather hide.
- 16"W x12"H x 5"D. Easily fits both laptop and plenty of space for documents or folders.
- Satchels, Cross-Body Bags, Shoulder Bags.
- Double stitched. Padded interior central section for laptop protection. Three spacious interior compartments.
- Stylish classic round corner finish. Stitched front pocket. Heavy duty burnished brass buckles and rivets throughout. Interior zipper compartments for added security. Traditionally hand made. Ethically produced.

I like this one too, as it clearly states the various USPs and the bullet points are excellent:

Salter Detachable Handle Ceramic Coated Multi-Function Saucepan Set

Ideal for a new home, these Salter pans are the perfect starter set, including three saucepans and a detachable handle, which enables you to store one pan inside the other, saving space in your cupboard. Made from forged aluminium with ceramic-coated interiors, they are suitable for the hob, oven, fridge and dishwasher. Use the pan alone to cook in the oven or simply attach the handle if you wish to use on the hob, then place a heat proof mat on your table and serve dinner straight from the pan.

- This set consists of 16, 18 and 20 cm saucepans, flat glass lids with steaming vents and a detachable black TPR soft touch handle.
- With an orange degraded enamel effect exterior, the saucepans look great and will add a fabulous splash of colour to your kitchen.
- As well as being suitable for all hob types, the pans are safe to use in the oven up to 200 so you can cook a huge range of dishes.
- Amazingly convenient to use, they can even be cleaned in the dishwasher, so you can enjoy cooking without the hassle of washing up.
- The handle is detachable, so you can simply place the smaller pans inside the larger one for a handy space saving storage solution.

Offer

This is where you enter your selling price. You can also add a sale price too. Both of these can be changed at any time.

More details

Under this tab are various boxes, many of which won't be relevant to what you're selling. Here's a summary:
- Your price.
- Product Dimensions and Weight – You need to enter these accurately as it's from these details that Amazon calculates your storage and shipping fees.

- Launch Date – It's definitely worth adding a launch date, if you know it. You can also add this date when your listing comes live, so your customers know it's a new product.
- Other Sections – There are countless other boxes you can fill in depending on your product. For example, if you're selling electrical products you'll need to complete the Power Source box. As you scroll down the page, you'll see that it's pretty self-explanatory.

Selling variations

If you have multiple versions of the same product, for example different colour or different size, you're obliged to sell them under the same listing. This has many advantages, not least that you'll be able to get more reviews allocated to one product. Note: Not all product categories allow for product variations, but this is becoming less of a problem, as Amazon is constantly increasing/improving variation options.

The main product information, such as images, product description and features will appear in all variations of the product you want to sell.

In Amazon speak, you're creating a "parent/child" relationship – all variations include a parent and a number of unique children. The parent is basically a non-buyable "umbrella" that connects the different variation children. For example, your parent could be T-shirt (note: T-shirt is a generic non-descriptive term) and the children could include: small white T-shirt, medium white T-shirt, large white T-shirt, small red T-shirt, medium red T-shirt, large red T-shirt etc.

Once you've created your basic product listing, click on the "Variation" tab and select all the appropriate "Variation Themes" (e.g. size or colour or both) from the drop-down menu, including all the possible variations that you may include at a later date.

Top tip: Make sure you get this right as it can't be changed, although, you can change the variations within your chosen theme/themes. So, for example, if you chose "Size" as your theme, you could add "Extra Small" at a later date. (Nonetheless, it makes sense to add all the possible variations now, as this will make your life easier down the line.)

Once you have chosen your variation themes, you can then add the variations. So, for example, if your variation theme was size you can then add all the different sizes. You will need a different barcode (EAN) number for each variant. Don't worry about filling in the "Seller SKU" box, as Amazon will automatically generate this for you. Before you click "Save and Finish" you'll also need to add "The Condition", "Your Price" and "Quantity".

Delivering to Amazon's fulfilment centres

While poring over Amazon FBA blogs and free Kindle FBA books, you're bound to come across the term drop-ship (or drop-shipping). In the Amazon FBA context, this means you're providing goods by direct delivery from the manufacturer to the retailer (i.e. Amazon.co.uk).

To arrange the drop-shipping of your stock, click on "Inventory" and then "Manage Inventory". Select the relevant product and from the right-hand dropdown list select "Send/Replenish Inventory". You can now create a shipping plan.

The first time you do this you'll probably feel like giving up – it's a tedious, cumbersome, unintuitive process. But it does get easier with practice and the numerous "What's this?" links are pretty helpful.

In summary, you will need the following to create the shipping plan:
- The full name, address, phone number and fax number of your supplier.
- The number of units you're sending.
- The number of boxes (cartons) you're sending.
- The weight of each box.
- The size of each box (cm x cm x cm).

Once you've created the plan, you will be issued with a unique Shipment ID and box (carton) labels.

These labels are crucial. Each one has a unique barcode that enables Amazon's fulfilment centre to identify your products. Any unlabeled delivery will be turned away.

You need to send the carton labels to your supplier so they can stick them on the cartons. There are numerous shipping requirements. Here are some of the key points:

- Each box must be limited to contain only one Shipment ID.
- Each box should weigh no more than 23kg, unless it contains one single oversized item that exceeds 23kg. Boxes weighing more than 15kg must be marked "Heavy Package" (viewable from both the top and sides of each heavy-weight container).
- Cartons weighing more than 23kg must be broken down into smaller shipment weights.
- Carton dimensions should not exceed 63.5 cm on any side, unless the dimension of a single deliverable unit exceeds 63.5 cm in itself.
- Boxes must not be bagged or covered in stretch wrap.
- Boxes must not be covered in packing tape as this prevents them from being able to be recycled.
- Neither point-of-sale containers nor bulk boxes may be used for delivery.
- Boxes must be packaged so that the contents can withstand the rigours of transportation and processing at Amazon Fulfilment Centres.

However, I urge you to read Amazon's guidance on FBA shipping and routing requirements and share them with your supplier: https://sellercentral.amazon.co.uk/gp/help/help.html?itemID=G2001415 10&language=en_GB

Top tip: Get your supplier to attach the delivery label to the top and the side of the box (away from the seams).

You should also instruct your supplier to:

- Ensure the courier bills you for VAT and import duty. If you don't, customs may well try to collect the VAT and import duty from Amazon, which isn't going to happen.
- Ensure they separate "cost of goods" and "delivery costs" on the air waybill (AWB) to make sure VAT and import duty is not charged on shipping costs.

You can track the status of your shipment. Here are the various stages:
- Working - You have not sent the shipment.
- Ready to Ship - You have entered the required information in the shipping workflow but you haven't clicked "Mark as Shipped".
- Shipped - You have clicked "Mark as Shipped". At this point you should add the courier tracking number, which you will need to obtain from your supplier. You should also ask them for an estimated delivery date.
- In-Transit - The shipment has been reported in-transit to one of Amazon's fulfilment centres.
- Delivered - The shipment has been reported as delivered to one of Amazon's fulfilment centres.
- Checked-In - The shipment has been checked-in to a dock at one of Amazon's fulfilment centres.
- Receiving - The shipment contents are being processed into inventory. This process may be delayed if incorrect quantities or improperly labeled items have been sent.
- Closed - All of the inventory in your shipment has been processed and is available for fulfilment. Happy days! Pop that champagne cork.

Top tip: Amazon fulfilment centres are notoriously fussy. They will refuse to accept any deliveries that are not 100% correctly packaged, labelled etc. To overcome this, I use Regional Express (https://www.regionalexpress.co.uk), who are a UK-based freight forwarder - not least because they have a division experienced in delivering to Amazon's fulfilment centres. Alternatively, if you want guaranteed success, use Amazon's Partnered Carrier Programme. When you're creating your shipping plan, in the Delivery Service section you will see the option to use an Amazon partnered carrier. For more details, click on this link: https://sellercentral.amazon.co.uk/gp/help/help.html/ref=sc_hp_rel_201119120?ie=UTF8&itemID=201119120&language=en_GB&ld=NSGoogle_null

It's now time to start promoting your products. But before you do that, this is a great time to review your pricing to make sure you're not doing yourself a disservice.

Pricing your products

In the economic theory of perfect competition there's an assumption of perfect knowledge, whereby consumers are assumed to know, among other things, price, functionality and quality. And, with some research, the Internet has made this theory a reality. As shoppers become increasingly Internet savvy, it's much harder to charge higher prices for the same product. I recently spoke to a wine merchant in London whose margins had dropped almost 5% over the last ten years (from 14% to 9%). He specialises in fine and rare wines, which are now far easier to track down online. Gone are the days of 100% markup.

In addition, as you know, Alibaba is the go-to website for sourcing goods. This can cause problems too. If you buy "off the shelf" products that are readily available, you haven't added value. I noticed that Jamie Oliver's team buys much of its kitchenware from Alibaba suppliers. They don't change the products, but instead add Jamie's name to them. Some of the selling prices are ten times the original purchase price! I'll leave you to be the judge of that. However, he's got an existing brand: Jamie Oliver. What have you got? (And, in fairness to Jamie, he seems like a good guy, who gives lots of his time and money to charity.)

If you want to charge higher prices you need your own products with your own designs and your own brand. This is not as daunting as it sounds. I'm not suggesting reinventing the wheel, merely improving products and rebranding them. And if you need designers or illustrators there are plenty available on Fiverr. But, you may be better off speaking to the manufacturer. The good ones will work with a wide range of creative industries. I found a hugely talented and lovely illustrator this way.

Once you have settled on your product, brand name and logo, you can start to get to the nitty-gritty of setting a price. I'm going to assume you want to make money on each item you sell. (This is not always the case, as some people are willing to sacrifice short-term profits for long-term growth – in fact, isn't that what Amazon did for years?!). To guarantee a profit you need to price your products using Cost Plus Pricing. In other words, add up all your costs and then add an additional sum of money. You can then work out your profit margin.

Costs to take into account

In this section I have not included time costs. If you're reading this book, you're probably not on someone else's clock, unless you're moonlighting. But time is imponderably important. It probably took me 50 hours of work to get my first FBA product listed. On top of that, I had spent time creating the brand name, the logo, the Facebook page and the website. So there's a big up-front cost in terms of time. However, when the first batch sold out, the re-order took less than two hours.

Good record keeping is essential – set up a spreadsheet and keep a record of every penny you spend. As you grow, you might want to invest in some accountancy software, such as QuickBooks. Below is a list of some of the main costs you're likely to incur:
- Set up costs – As mentioned above, setting up a new brand costs money. You don't have to allocate this against your first product, but you should be aware of it.
- Product development costs – You may have to pay for designers or for samples (or for both). These are necessary costs, and should be divided by the number of units you order. For example, if your sample cost £60 and you order 120 units, you should add 50p per unit to cover this. Unless, that is, you can get the manufacturer to refund the sample fee when you order in bulk.

- Packaging costs – Including packaging materials, branding and barcoding. Get the supplier to quote for this sooner rather than later, otherwise they can end up being an unpleasant surprise when you come to pay the bill.
- Barcode costs – Not a huge amount, but not to be ignored, especially when you're just starting out. The cost per barcode is much higher on small orders.
- Purchase price (FOB) – Initially this price is likely to be higher as you test the water with your product. Assuming you buy in larger quantities when you reorder, the cost per unit should drop.
- Shipping costs – The main factors affecting these are the weight and volume of the shipment. Also, if you're in a rush, expect to pay more.
- Import duty – As per your commodity code.
- VAT on your imports – That adds 20% to your largest input cost. Ouch!
- VAT on your sales – I've registered for a flat rate of tax, so pay 7.5% VAT but can't claim VAT back on purchases. What VAT arrangements you make are up to you. If you're unsure, seek professional advice. However, you should be aware that if, during the course of any 12 months, your taxable supplies exceed the VAT registration threshold (£85,000), you are legally obliged to register for VAT.
- FBA costs – This is what you pay Amazon and covers storage, referral fee, packaging and postage. This is calculated using a number of factors including the type of product, the weight and the size. (FBA costs are explained in detail later on in this chapter.)
- Communication costs – I've assumed that you already have a mobile phone, a laptop/tablet and access to the Internet. As such, it's up to you whether you include these costs. Below I have detailed a few apps that fellow FBAers use to help keep their costs down.

Whatsapp – This text-message app uses your data package (or WiFi) instead of depleting your message allowance. This means you can send text, images or videos anywhere in the world for free. It's now the most common method of sending messages. To get the best use, always send your messages via WhatsApp – your contacts will then start doing the same.

Skype, WhatsApp and FaceTime – There are many apps that allow you to make phone calls anywhere in the world for free. Skype, WhatsApp and FaceTime are three of the best. You'll need to be in a WiFi zone, a small price to pay for "free".

Google translate - Google's app supports over 100 languages. A must if you're struggling to communicate with a supplier. The app's accuracy is improving all the time – Google's Translate Community has contributed millions of corrected translations and words.

PDF scanner – Turn your mobile into a scanner with one of the many PDF-scanner apps. This is a very handy app if you do a lot of work away from your home or office. I use GeniusScan and it's great!

Dropbox – Another great app for those working on the go. Save and access your files from the cloud. There are lots of other cloud storage options, for example the Google Drive (which gives you 15GB of free storage).

Amazon fees

There are a number of variables that affect how much you pay, including:
- Type of product: non-media, media or oversize.
- Type of sales channel: Amazon.co.uk, internationally or another channel.

The fees are made up of:

Per-item fee
This is a flat-rate fee of £0.75 + VAT (unless you have a Professional Seller Account, in which case you pay £25 + VAT per month).

Referral fees
These range from 7% to 15%, with one exception: Amazon device accessories (e.g. Kindle accessories) clock in at a breathtaking 45%.

For full details on referral fees, click here: https://services.amazon.co.uk/services/sell-online/pricing.html and then select "Seller Central Fee Schedule".

Variable closing fee
These are also flat-rate fees that range from 14p to £1.15, but are only levied on the following: books, music, DVDs and VHS videos (do people still buy VHS videos?).

Fulfilment fees
These are the fees Amazon charges for picking, packing and posting. They are most affected by the size and weight of the item.

Storage fees
Amazon also charges for storing your FBA stock. The fees are per cubic foot per month and different product categories are charged different amounts. This is worth bearing in mind, particularly if you're selling light but bulky items. In fact, these charges can be ruinous if you have a static stock. "Clothing, Shoes and Bags" for example, incur the following storage fees:
January to September = £0.39
October to December = £0.55

Many of Amazon's fees change regularly. Click here to get the latest: https://m.media-amazon.com/images/G/02/FBA_Files/2019/191111-FBA-Rate-Card-UK.pdf?ld=NSGoogle_null

Top tip: Working out FBA fees manually can be time consuming. I tend to fill in all the relevant details when listing the product and Amazon then calculate the fee. I then adjust my selling price according to this.

Long-term storage fees

In addition to monthly storage fees, Amazon also charges long-term storage fees based on the total volume in cubic feet of units that have been stored in Amazon fulfilment centres for more than 365 days. FBAers are charged a monthly long-term storage fee of £4.30 per cubic foot or a minimum fee of £0.10 per unit.

For more details, click here:
https://sellercentral.amazon.co.uk/gp/help/help.html?itemID=G200684750&language=en_GB

Top tip: Be careful not to order too much stock.

Re-ordering

Re-ordering is usually a straightforward affair. But it's also an opportunity to put right anything that was wrong with the previous order. One issue I've encountered is my contact leaving. When this happened, I ended up drafting an email that covered everything I could think of. Over time, it morphed into a template (see below), which I've used numerous times. Feel free to use it too – you're welcome!

Dear << >>

I hope this email finds you well. I've almost sold out of the << >> that you kindly supplied last year. As such, I'd like to order some more please.

Hopefully this email will provide you with most of the details you require:

- Could I please order the same << >> as before (see attached Word document to remind you of the designs)?
- << >> of each design please.
- Please put four << >> (one of each design) into the packaging.
- Packaging – using polythene packaging you usually use to pack pillow cores – taped/sealed with barcode labels.

- The barcode label is attached.
- Would it be possible to add a label to each << >> to include:
  - Washing instructions (in English).
  - A << >> logo (attached).

Could you please provide me with a FOB price for these << >> and delivery costs? Also, could you please provide payment details?

Delivery:
- Could you please separate the "cost of goods" and "delivery costs" on the air waybill (AWB)?
- As before, I will need these delivered to Amazon in the UK. I will forward you the delivery label when I have it. In order to obtain this label, I will need you to supply me the following information:
  - Number of cartons being delivered.
  - Number of items in each carton.
  - Size of each carton - cm x cm x cm.
  - Weight of each carton.
- In the meantime, could you please provide the following information:
  - Packaged product weight and dimensions (per set of four << >>).
  - Please confirm your address and telephone number.

Other useful information/requests:
- My EORI number is: << >>.
- Could you please make sure the courier knows to invoice me directly for import duty and VAT?
- My up-to-date contact details are: <<name, address, phone number, email address>>.
- Commodity code: << >>.

When dispatched, could you please:
- Provide me with a tracking number/name of the courier.

I look forward to hearing from you.

Thank you in advance for your help.

In this piece of communication, I have:
- Provided the supplier with everything they need to complete the order.
- Created a checklist for myself.

Customer reviews

Customer reviews are crucial. Review rates vary product to product, but most estimates suggest that less than 5% of buyers review products. However, over 20% of buyers reviewed the first product I sold on Amazon. I managed this by contacting all my customers after they bought the product. Things have got much harder since then, it should be noted. Amazon now allows buyers to opt out of receiving unsolicited messages from sellers. There is no published data on the numbers, but my own research suggests over 50% of regular Amazon shoppers have done so.

To contact your customers (who have not opted out of being contacted): Click on "Orders", "Manage Orders" and then the customer's name.

Here's a copy of the email I sent my fifth ever customer:

Dear Linda

Thanks for buying our cushion covers. You're our fifth ever customer – we're a very new business – and your custom is hugely appreciated.

I hope the covers arrived safely and you're happy with them.

Assuming you are, we would be very grateful if you could write a product review on Amazon.

(If you have experienced any problems, please do get in touch.)

Thank you in advance for your help.

In this piece of communication, I have:
- Personalised the email.
- Thanked them for their custom.
- Told them we're a new company – people want start-ups to do well.
- Asked them to get in touch should they have encountered any issues.

This final point may well be the most important. It effectively stops people posting negative reviews. Admittedly, on occasion, I've ended up going beyond the call of duty in terms of customer service. However, in the long run, I think this is worthwhile.

I send this email a few days after the item has been dispatched. If the customer hasn't reviewed, I will send a follow-up about a week later. Some people advocate sending a second follow-up, but I don't want to pester my customers, so I don't. Well, unless I'm desperate for reviews.

And reviews work: Research published in the Review of Reviews suggested that almost 84% of consumers trusted users' reviews over critics' reviews.

I don't see any harm in asking friends and family to write your initial reviews provided they are honest reviews. And I wouldn't advocate promoting your products overtly until you have at least one positive review. Do not pay strangers to write reviews. This is not allowed and could result in your products being delisted.

Once your business grows, you can automate your feedback request emails. FeedbackFive (www.ecomengine.com/feedbackfive) and Feedbackz (www.feedbackz.com) offer this service to Amazon's UK sellers. But try to keep requests as personal as possible – nowadays people are constantly being asked for feedback and are therefore selective about when they write positive reviews. And don't forget, Brits love to complain!

Top tip: include a "request to review" card with your product. A small printed card will suffice. This is inexpensive and, yet, surprisingly effective. Some people also include a small gift – I received free seeds with some gardening products I purchased. Haribos go down well too. As did tea bags and biscuits, as I once received with a kitchen I ordered online – they kept the builders very happy.

Verified reviews vs. unverified reviews

An unverified review is where Amazon doesn't have a record of that person buying the product, but they left a review anyway. A verified review is one where the customer bought the product through Amazon and used the same Amazon account to leave a review. Verified reviews are definitely better. But, most customers don't know the difference between the verified reviews and unverified reviews.

Bad reviews – Grrr!

It can take months to build up a bank of good reviews, only for one person to spoil everything. It's part of the business - everyone receives bad reviews. Sometimes they will be awful, unfair and untrue. Don't let them cause you sleepless nights – the Internet has long been the domain of the troll. Baseless rants may affect your star rating, but many users look at the one- and two-star reviews too – and they will see through senseless tirades. Make sure you bury them with loads of five-star reviews. And sometimes it's not even your fault – Amazon Logistics has been responsible for a few of mine.

On the other hand, some negative reviews are completely legitimate. If the criticism is constructive, use it to improve your products.

However, if the review is blatantly unjust, you have two choices:

- Write to the customer and ask them to amend/take down the review.
- Ask Amazon to remove the review.

Writing to customers

Sometimes negative customer reviews feel personal – they're not. Likewise, your criticism of their review may sting too. As such, you need to tread carefully. Don't email them straight away. Instead, give yourself time to cool down; this will give them time to cool down too.

Here's an example of what you could write:

Dear << >>

I just read your negative feedback – ouch! The product description clearly stated the << >> was made from a cotton linen mix. As such, I think leaving a negative review stating "not 100% cotton" is a little unfair.

As such I'd be very grateful if you could reconsider the negative feedback. It's very difficult competing with large corporations – we're a small business and customer reviews are our lifeblood.

In addition, you can obtain a full refund if you return the << >> free of charge using an Amazon pre-paid postage label. Please get in touch if you need help with this process.

Thank you in advance for your help.

Responding to negative reviews publicly

Responding publicly may add fuel to the fire, so make sure you're on firm ground before you post anything. In fact, as I've learned to my detriment, it's probably best avoided!

Ask Amazon to remove the review

When I first attempted this, it took me almost an hour to fathom it out. Amazon doesn't make it easy to contact them, that's for sure.

Here's what you need to do: Open your Amazon Seller Central page, scroll down to the bottom and on the left hand side you'll see a small "Get support" link. Click on it. Select "Request Customer Feedback Removal" and then click on "Feedback Manager". From then on it's plain sailing.

Amazon officially lists only a handful of reasons they'll remove reviews, for example those containing obscenities. But, it would seem you can get reviews removed for numerous reasons including:

- Personal information – If the review contains a name, email address, URL or phone number.
- Product review confused with seller feedback – Many customers don't know the difference. If the customer has obviously left their comments in the wrong section, you have grounds to appeal.
- Fake reviews, including those posted by your competitors.
- Numerous negative reviews from one unhappy customer.
- One-word reviews.
- Price objections - In 2013 Amazon started to agree to remove price feedback such as, "You can buy this for less at Tesco".
- The review contains details about where else to buy the product.
- It's not an original review – I.e. the text has been copied from elsewhere.
- Using feedback as an email - For example, "I thought this product came with batteries. Could you please send the batteries?"
- Demonstrably untrue – It's not uncommon for customers to complain about something that was clearly stated in the product description. For example, "This product is not

Bluetooth compatible". If the description stated clearly this was the case, appeal.

- Irrelevant comment – For example, "I wish these came in Pillarbox Red". That's as maybe, but they ordered them in orange.
- We did nothing wrong – For example, the customer requests delivery to an incorrect address and then complains that it's been sent to the wrong place.
- FBA sales – If, in Amazon's own words, "The entire feedback comment is about fulfilment or customer service for an order fulfilled by Amazon."

When contacting Amazon, clearly and politely state your issue and request an action (i.e. that they remove the review). There is no guarantee Amazon will remove the review but, if you don't ask, you don't get.

Amazon Vine

Lots of you may have read about this programme that allows "a select group of Amazon customers to post opinions about new and pre-release items to help their fellow customers make educated purchasing decisions."

Basically Amazon invites people to join this panel based on the quality and quantity of their reviews. This programme caused some ire. Amazon selects the reviewers and the vendors have to pay to get their products listed. And, it's only available to those who sell on the Vendor Central platform. Worse still, there are new rules that make getting reviews even harder.

Customer review rules

As of October 2016, Amazon started cracking down on the practice of offering free or discounted products in exchange for reviews. Its reasons are admirable: ReviewMeta's study of more than seven million reviews found that the average rating for products with incentivised reviews was higher than those for non-incentivised ones. But, why then do they still have their Vine programme? Rank hypocrisy, if you ask me.

Their new rules state, "Creating, modifying, or posting content in exchange for compensation of any kind (including free or discounted products) is not allowed".

Amazon has flexed its muscles too: it has sued companies who it claimed had paid people for reviews. It has also taken legal action against thousands of people who offer to submit positive reviews in return for payment.

You have been warned.

The dark arts of Amazon Search Engine Optimization (SEO)

Amazon sells over 300 million products. This long-tail model is great for Amazon as it's a sure-fire way of satisfying its customers' wants and needs. It's also why Amazon is often referred to as The Everything Store. However, for sellers, that means a potentially daunting number of competitors. There are over 40,000 results for "cycle helmet" alone. You can partially overcome this by finding a niche, having a strong brand or a compelling USP.

But how do you get onto the first page and why is it important?

Amazon doesn't publish data on typical customer habits, but data has been published for Google – and 96% of Google users don't go beyond page one. It's safe to assume that it's similar for Amazon. After all, Amazon is effectively a product "search engine".

So, if you're not on the first page it's much harder to make significant sales.

There are some exceptions though. Customers can sort by "Avg. Customer Review", "Price", "Newest arrivals" and "Featured" (as well as the default setting of "Relevance"). Perversely, having the highest price could be an advantage, as some customers are looking for premium products. A low price helps too. New listings get a boost – but not for long as hundreds of new products are added every day.

Note: Customers often filter by "Prime" - yet another reason to use FBA.

The main factors that affect your ranking

- As discussed before, the number and quality of your customer reviews will push up your ranking.

- Volume of sales – Amazon wants to make money - no surprise there. But remember, sales rank doesn't always correlate with the keywords used in searches, but rather how high they are within a certain category.

- High conversion rates – Amazon loves searches that result in sales – they want products that people buy to rank highly. They're not interested in window-shopping products. Here's a summary of how you can improve conversion rates:
  - Great product title.
  - A range of high-resolution pictures.
  - A compelling product description.
  - Branded products.
  - Detailed bullet points.
  - Customer reviews.
  - Note: If you want to see your page visits, sales and conversion rate, click on "Reports", "Business Report", "Detailed Page Sales and Traffic".

- Price – Needless to say, if you sell your product at a compelling price people are more likely to convert (i.e. buy). But I am loath to spend too much time on this point. In almost all Amazon SEO guides/articles/blogs etc. price features prominently. But it's not an insight; it's common sense. Plus, focusing on ever-lowering prices is classic race-to-the-bottom economics. This is particularly the case when there are a number of sellers of the same product. Sooner or later you'll end up selling at a loss. Focus on your brand and your USP and you're far more likely to make a profit. However, there's nothing wrong with keeping your price as low as possible, especially if you're new to the market. This loss-leader strategy can be used to get your conversion rates up and increase the number of customer reviews. You can then increase the price. But, don't forget, the rules of supply and demand apply. Some products will be price elastic others will be price inelastic. Obviously, if you're the only supplier, your products are more likely to be price inelastic. This is even more likely if there are no close substitute products.

· Keywords – Try to get your keywords into the title and "search terms". But, before you do this, you need to identify the best keywords. The Merchant Words website (www.merchantwords.com) allows you to find the words that people search for before buying Amazon's products. If money is tight, check out Google Keywords Planner (adwords.google.co.uk/KeywordPlanner) and type in your product name to identify related searches.

Keywords top tips

- Your product will only appear in a search if you have included ALL the keywords in the customer's search query. You can put lots of these in the title and your bullet-points. However, you should definitely include them in your keywords search term boxes (especially if you have been unable to include them elsewhere).
- Some keywords are not suitable for "public consumption", for example, common misspellings (e.g. Guiness) or slang. Make sure you add these to your keywords too.

- Each of the five "Search Terms" sections allows up to 1,000 characters – that's 5,000 characters. Fill them with as many unique, relevant keywords as you can.
- Avoid repetitions by using hyphenated keywords. For example, the keyword "body-firming" will also pick up "body firming", "bodyfirming", "body" and "firming".
- Don't worry about including singular and plural words – both are automatically included in the search. Same goes for uppercase and lowercase.
- Avoid "filler words" such as "and" – These aren't counted as keywords and will not be picked up.
- Separate keywords with a space – Full stops and commas are not required. In fact, avoid all punctuation. Things such as exclamation marks (e.g. 100% cotton!) next to words are potentially disastrous, as your product won't be listed unless the search includes the exclamation mark. And, who searches for "cotton!"?

To enter your keywords, go to Seller Central, click on "Inventory" then "Manage Inventory" and then "Edit" (to the right of your product listing). Under the "Keywords" tab enter your keywords in the "Search Terms" section.

Amazon SEO rumours

Amazon's search algorithm is called A9. Unless they're hacked it's unlikely to enter the public domain any time soon. And, even if it did, it would undoubtedly take some time to decode. So, for now, we're left with third party research, snippets from Amazon and guesswork. As such, there are various unproven theories, which I've listed below. I can't prove they're true, but I'm also unable to disprove them.

- Amazon's SEO places far more emphasis on verified reviews (as opposed to unverified reviews). This makes sense. But I have yet to see data that backs up this claim.

- Number of answered questions. Under each product listing is a "Customer Questions & Answers" section. This is where potential customers can ask product questions. Initially you may need to answer product questions. But, as you get reviews, Amazon redirects any customer questions to previous reviewers. (Looking at these is also a great source of ideas to improve your product description and bullet points.)
- It has also been suggested that Amazon looks at defect rates (i.e. number of returned products).
- Time on page. Amazon tracks the amount of time customers spend on each page. The longer they spend, the more interested they are assumed to be. Having great photos, bullet points, descriptions and reviews all help to keep customers interested for longer.
- Exit rate. Do customers exit Amazon.co.uk after viewing your product? It's thought that Amazon takes this as a sign that you have a poor listing.
- There are a number of analysts who think running Amazon Sponsored Products advertising also improves a product's ranking. More on this later.
- In-stock rate. This isn't too relevant for FBA sellers. But make sure you have stock during busy periods.

Basic Seller or Professional Seller Account

Lots of FBA articles advocate switching to a Professional Seller once you're making 35 or more sales a month. However, few explain why. The financial reason is simple maths. To become a Professional Seller you pay £30 a month (i.e. £25 + VAT). However you don't pay the per-item seller fee of approx. £0.90 per sale. And, since £30/£0.90 = 33.33 the actual trigger point is roughly 34 items a month.

I usually recommend starting off with a Basic Seller account and only switching to a Professional Seller Account once you're selling 34+ items. Switching from one to another is very simple: Go to your Seller Account page. Click on "Settings" (top right) and select "Account Info.". On the left you'll see "Your Services" – click on "Manage". Then click on "Change Your Selling Plan". Read the terms and conditions then click "Proceed".

Products requiring prior approval

You need prior approval from Amazon to sell products in certain categories. This seems to change frequently, so click on the link at the bottom of this section to find the latest information. At the time of writing, the following categories required prior approval from Amazon: Toys & Games; Jewellery; Made in Italy; Music; DVD; Organic Foods; Organic Feed; Organic Pet Food; Beer; Wine & Spirits; Streaming Media Players and Watches.

Obtaining this approval tends to be reasonably straightforward you'll be pleased to hear.

If you want to sell one of these products, you'll be asked to answer a series of questions. Imagine you're doing a psychometric test – give them the answers they want to hear, including the fact you're planning on selling more than one item. Most applications are approved immediately, assuming you answer each question sensibly (e.g. don't say you're only planning on selling one product).

To learn more about how to sell restricted products on Amazon, click on this link: https://sellercentral.amazon.co.uk/gp/help/200333160

Promoting your products

This subject merits a book in its own right. Or, it would seem, several thousand – I know, I've read dozens of them. Instead of trying to replicate what's already out there, I've tried to summarise some useful hints and tips to get you started and hopefully to stimulate some further thoughts/ideas.

With your first product, start by emailing/texting your friends and family with the product link. Even if they're not interested themselves, they may forward your email/text.

Make use of your current social media profile – for example, Facebook, Instagram, Twitter, Snapchat or Pinterest – especially if you're launching a new business or a new range of products. TikTok is another platform to keep an eye on - it's growing fast.

These two things will help generate interest, but are unlikely to result in too many sales. And, if you're relying on selling to people you know, it's not a sustainable business.

I've tested a number of platforms for promoting products, including Google AdWords, Facebook/Instagram advertising and Amazon Sponsored Products advertising. The lowest cost per sale came via the latter. Facebook was about three times the cost and Google AdWords simply wasn't viable when promoting an individual product. (Had I done my research, I wouldn't have tested Google AdWords, given that three times as many buyers search for products to buy on Amazon.)

That's not to say you should then ditch Facebook/Instagram. They are great platforms to launch new products and to keep customers engaged. But, remember, if you're promoting products you'll need a Facebook business page. In simple terms, business pages get "likes" and personal pages get "friends". The great thing about Facebook is the simplicity. You have one account login and can easily switch between accounts.

Note: Facebook acquired Instagram in 2012 and Instagram now has over a billion active users. The good news for advertisers is that it's now possible to target Instagram users far more accurately.

Amazon Sponsored Products advertising

As I mentioned before, Amazon Sponsored Products advertising is a great way to get your products noticed, especially if you have a low organic ranking or don't feature on the first page in terms of Average Customer

Review. They are also very useful if you're selling seasonal products, are promoting a new offer (e.g. reduced price), want to shift slow-moving stock or have a unique product to sell.

Amazon Sponsored Products advertising is Pay Per Click (PPC), so it's highly accountable. And, being an online campaign, it's very flexible - you can amend it whenever you want (e.g. change the budget, pause, amend the keywords etc.).

Note: You have to own the "Buy Box" to use Amazon Sponsored Products advertising. That's sensible - otherwise you risk promoting your competitors' products.

To get started, head to Seller Central, click on "Advertising" and then "Campaign manager". At this point, you will need to choose:
·   Campaign name.
·   Automated or manual key words.
·   Start date and end date.
·   Daily budget.
·   Starting bid (i.e. the maximum amount you are willing to pay when someone clicks your advert).

Take time to name each campaign so they're easily identifiable – when you have numerous campaigns running it can soon get confusing.

Amazon Sponsored Products advertisements are based on keywords, which can be entered manually or by using Amazon's automatic targeting tool. The latter matches the shopper's query to your existing product keywords, and is probably the better option for your first campaign for any product. That's assuming, of course, your product information keywords are on the money.

Top tip: If you have been running an automatic keyword campaign for a while, click on the blue "Download Search Term report" link (you'll find this by clicking on your campaign's name). This allows you to see all the search terms that resulted in at least one click to your advert. As such, based on this data, you may decide, in the future, to switch to manual targeting with refined keywords.

You can set an open-ended end date, but only do this if you're planning on checking your reports reasonably regularly. In terms of your daily budget, start with a small amount and assess the results at the end of the month. Assuming there's a positive Return On Investment (ROI) you can then ramp it up to take advantage of this.

Also, like Facebook and Google AdWords, Amazon Sponsored Products adverts are set up like an auction. In other words, you have to "bid" for how much you're willing to pay for someone to click on your advert – Amazon call this the "Starting Bid". But how much to bid? If you click on the name of your campaign, you'll see the "suggested bid" – this is a good start point. If you need to shift stock, you may decide to bid a little above this amount.

Amazon Sponsored Products adverts seem to take a few weeks to gather momentum. I can only assume that this is because people add products to their Wish List (or other lists) and then purchase your product at a later date. When you start to make sales, Amazon will automatically lower your PPC due to higher conversion rates. Also, as I mentioned briefly before, there is also some evidence to suggest running Amazon Sponsored Products adverts improves your organic ranking – possibly as a result of increased visitors and higher sales.

Note: The campaign will get you eyeballs, but it won't get you sales. There is no point in running any advertising until your product page looks fantastic. To reiterate: that includes high-quality, high-resolution images, detailed product descriptions and, of course, some positive reviews.

Finally, just to be even-handed, I've noticed that some sellers are not keen on Amazon Sponsored Products advertising as they view them as purely another revenue stream for Amazon. And they do have a point. Amazon are, in effect, trying to out-Google Google by grabbing a share of the highly-lucrative search market. And it's their sellers who are paying.

So is Amazon being greedy? Probably. But if Amazon Sponsored Products advertising works for you, why cut off your nose to spite your face?

Paying for Amazon Sponsored Products advertising

Advertisers can pay their fees from the proceeds in their seller account or via credit card or debit card. The upside of the former is that you don't have to update your cards if they expire (or are lost or stolen).

For more information, click on this link: https://services.amazon.co.uk/services/sponsored-products/how-it-works.html

Facebook/Instagram for business

Facebook provides lots of useful information to help you get the most out of your business pages: www.facebook.com/business. It's well worth reading this guide and the associated case studies. In the meantime, here are some top tips for the uninitiated:

- Fill your business page with relevant content (including the "about" section, which should include a "call to action" – e.g. encourage them to click on a link). If you have a unique brand name, that will help people find your Facebook page.
- Create an Instagram page and link this to your Facebook page. It's easy to post content on both platforms simultaneously.
- Promote your page – Initially, invite your existing Facebook friends to like your page. You should also email and text everyone you know to like your page. Use your other social networks too. Add the Facebook link to your website and below your email sign-off.
- Targeting the right people is essential – The image, headline, text and call to action are important too. But you should spend as much time making sure you reach the right people. Facebook allows you to target customers by:

- Location – Including country, city and postcode.
- Demographics – Including age, gender and education.
- Interests – Facebook identify these in a number of ways, including customers' own lists of interests and groups to which they belong.
- Behaviours – Including purchasing and device-usage behaviour.
- Custom audiences – There are lots of ways to use this. The most effective are "lookalike" audiences. In other words, Facebook creates an audience that looks like your current customers. However, there are two snags. Firstly, you have to have at least 100 customer records (and that's the absolute minimum). And, secondly, Amazon no longer makes your customer email addresses available to you, so it's much harder to create a datafile that enables Facebook to match your existing customers with their user database. If you can overcome these barriers, lookalike audiences should produce a better return on investment.
- Content is king – Post content that's engaging, interesting, memorable, newsworthy and shareable. Apparently over four million posts and adverts are liked on Facebook every minute – that's a lot! The top things people tend to share include: infographics, images, videos, interactive, list posts and quotes. People love to be part of something new (and to be "in the know"). That's worth bearing in mind. Better still, if you're able to involve customers (and potential customers) in business decisions, do. Why not create an interactive poll to help you choose which product to launch next?
- Boost your posts - If you're launching a new product, it's definitely worth paying to boost your new-product-launch posts. How much you spend depends on your budget. (If money is tight, re-post each post at least three times to improve coverage.)
- Schedule posts for downtime - Early morning, between work and dinner, and before bedtime. If you do this, your posts will be more widely read and shared. Note: Apparently Tuesday is the best day for shares.

- Engage – Acknowledge all customer engagement with a response, even if you're just "liking" their post. Social media is called social for a reason.
- Facebook Insights - This analytics tool allows you to analyse the performance of your various Facebook pages and campaigns. Use this data to refine and enhance your future campaigns.
- Have a call to action – For example, make sure your "Shop now" button links to your Amazon page or your website. If you don't tell people what to do, they'll soon drift away.
- Competitions – Running a competition can help generate a new audience and spread brand awareness. But people are cynical too; make sure you post a picture of the winner and explain exactly how the winner was chosen.

Other promotional ideas

Find the bloggers – The great thing about bloggers is that they are invariably more approachable than traditional journalists. Find the relevant ones with the most followers. There are cosmetics bloggers, fashion bloggers, homeware bloggers etc. – find the ones you'd like to write about your product, send them a polite email offering a free sample etc. Make their lives easier too, by sending them JPEGs and the product page link.

Influencers - According to the dictionary, an influencer is a "person with the ability to influence potential buyers of a product or service by promoting or recommending the items on social media." So, that's good news. But influencers want to make money. Or, at the very least, get free products. Anyone with over 10,000 followers on Instagram will probably want cold hard cash before they post anything commercial. As an aside, anyone with a million plus followers on Instagram can charge £10,000 or more for each post. Assuming that's not an option, look for the up-and-coming influencers - those with less than 10,000 followers. Send them some free products. It's a small price to pay.

Infiltrate the online forums – But be careful not to break the rules. People who repeatedly post commercial content are often removed.

Forums can also be great places to get product ideas. If someone posts, "Does anyone make non-slip yoga socks?" and the answer is a resounding "No", that's your next product!

If you're launching an innovative product, consider sending out a press release. You can employ people on Fiverr to draft the content and others to obtain the email addresses of the journalists you'd like to target.

YouTube videos – If your product moves, make that movie. Show your remote control helicopter dive bombing pigeons. Post this promotional video on your social media platforms.

Create your own website – If you're selling multiple products, this becomes increasingly important. You can link them all to your product page on Amazon. WordPress and their various competitors are becoming increasingly intuitive – you can do it, you know you can. Personally, I'm a big fan of Squarespace.

Pinterest – The great thing about Pinterest is that it's primarily image based and has a strong bias towards things you can buy. And you can add a "Buy" button. If you're new to Pinterest I urge you to check out this article: https://blog.hootsuite.com/how-to-use-pinterest-for-business/

Twitter – I can't help but think that this isn't a great tool for business. And I read a whole book on the subject - *How To Twitter For Business Success*. But maybe I'm missing something - that book has a load of five-star reviews. Or maybe the author has just sussed out the Amazon review system? But I guess if you have a lot of followers, it's great. It's also very useful if you can get influencers to tweet about your product/products. A friend recently saw an upsurge in book sales when an influential author tweeted a positive review of his book.

You can also apply to have your product as part of Amazon's Lightning Deals – these are time-bound, promotional offers that allow your products to appear on Amazon Deals' page. All proposed Lightning Deals require Amazon's approval and attract a fee. HotUKdeals.com feature

these products too, which can help you gain additional publicity. Click here for more details:
www.amazon.co.uk/gp/help/customer/display.html?nodeId=200543730

Amazon money-off promotions

Amazon allow you to run two different types of promotion on their platform:
- · Money off.
- · Buy One Get One Free (BOGOF).

To qualify, customers have to meet a minimum threshold set by you – either monetary or based on the number of products purchased.

Money off

You can configure this offer in almost any way you want. For example, spend £12 or more, and get £2 off the purchase of qualifying products. Or, spend £12 or more, and get 10% off the purchase of qualifying products. Or, buy four items or more, and get £2 off the purchase of qualifying products. Or, buy four items or more, and get 10% off the purchase of qualifying products. I could go on…

Buy One Get One Free (BOGOF)

UK consumers are very used to this kind of promotion, so it doesn't merit a long explanation. Although, it doesn't have to be "buy one" - it could be "buy two" etc. As with money off, you can configure this offer to best suit your needs. For example, buy two bottles of aftershave and get one free. Or, buy one bottle of aftershave and get one free.

To set up a promotion, click on "Inventory" and then "Manage Promotions". You'll then see the two promotional types – select the right one for you. The process is pretty straightforward.

Amazon Launchpad

Late in 2015, Amazon Launchpad opened for business in the UK. This marketplace is for start-ups to launch their products. Unfortunately, it's closed to everyday entrepreneurs. Instead, you need to be working with one of their approved "venture capitalists, accelerators, incubators or crowdfunding platforms". Those crowdfunding platforms include Crowdfunder and Crowdcube.

So, if you're seeking funding for your business and you want to sell something truly innovative, this is worth exploring further: www.amazon.co.uk/gp/launchpad/signup

Handmade at Amazon

As far as I can fathom, this is Amazon taking on Etsy – according to their website it lets "Artisans sell their handcrafted products directly to millions of Amazon customers all over the world." If these are the kind of goods you're selling, this could be the platform for you.

You have to apply to join Handmade at Amazon. And it's only open to, "Approved Artisans and Collaborative groups (for example, cooperatives, non-profit companies or charities)."

The advantages seem to be increased publicity, enhanced product pages, an opportunity to showcase your workmanship and the chance to create your own profile pages.

For more details, please click on this link:
https://services.amazon.co.uk/handmade.html

Sell on eBay, fulfil via FBA

It's possible to fulfil orders that have been placed on any platform using FBA. But there are some significant downsides. Before I detail those, here's how you do it:
- Go to Manage Inventory.
- Select the item (tick the box to the left).
- From the drop down "Action on 1 selected", choose "Create fulfilment order".

- You can then transcribe the customer's name, address, email address and phone number into the boxes provided.
- I'd recommend entering the PayPal reference in the order ID box. If you need to look up this order up later, this will you allow to find it easily.
- Click "Continue".
- On the next screen, check the details and click "Place order".

It's all very clever, but is it viable? The first issue is the additional time cost – you have to manually enter the customer's details. On top of that, these orders are not eligible for Prime. There's also the issue of customer perception – will customers query the Amazon packaging and labeling? For most people it won't matter, but some might find it odd. Also, Amazon does not provide customer service on these orders, so that's back in your court. Nor will they gift-wrap or deal with any returns. Worse still, it's more expensive.

Here's an example of what happens if you sell a typical item on eBay for £20 weighing 0.5kg, with free postage. (And, by the way, I strongly urge you to charge the same total price on all platforms – nothing annoys customers more than realising they could have got their item cheaper elsewhere.)

The cost of selling on eBay and fulfilling via FBA:

Amazon fulfilment fees =	£4.00
PayPal flat-rate fee =	£0.30
PayPal percentage fee @ 2.9% =	£0.58
eBay listing fee	£0.35
eBay sold fee @ 10% =	£2.00
Total	**£7.23**

Compare this to the FBA fee:

Amazon Referral Fee =	£3.60
FBA Fulfilment Fee =	£2.14
Total	**£5.74**

So, is this an option in any circumstance? The first questions to answer are: What are your margins? And will those additional fees eat up your profit? Assuming you can still make a profit, listing on eBay allows you to reach a new audience. This might be worth testing, especially if you're struggling to get noticed on Amazon. It also means you can sell on eBay without having stock cluttering your home and you can fulfil orders even if you're abroad.

Returns and damaged stock

Returns
Amazon.co.uk offers returns for most items within 30 days of receipt of delivery. There are some exceptions, but this policy covers the vast majority of its non-perishable inventory. For further details, click on this link:
www.amazon.co.uk/gp/help/customer/display.html/ref=hp_502480_top_rsp?nodeId=1161002

FBA Repackaging Service
Amazon has a free refurbishment service for all returned stock. Known as the FBA Repackaging Service, it was launched in November 2015. It's applied to all returns, which would normally be marked as customer damaged. Assuming the item can be sold again, as new, with a simple clean up and re-packaging, Amazon will undertake this task.

This used to be an opt-out service, but Amazon put a stop to this in September 2019. In other words, as a FBA seller, you will automatically be signed up to this service.

Lost and Damaged Inventory
When your inventory is either lost or damaged by Amazon, they will either:
  · Replace the item(s), or
  · Pay you the evaluated replacement value of your lost inventory, less any applicable FBA and selling-on-Amazon fees.
Assuming you're selling products unique to you, it's the latter that will apply. For further details, click here:
https://sellercentral.amazon.co.uk/gp/help/200213130?language=en_GB &ref=ag_200213130_cont_G201030350

Rules and regulations

Amazon listing rules
It's worth spending a few minutes reading these, not least because, if you breach them, you can be delisted. Click this link for more information:
https://sellercentral.amazon.co.uk/gp/help/help.html?itemID=G2003906 40&language=en_GB

Prohibited products
There are various products that you are not allowed to sell on the Amazon platform, few of which will surprise you. For example, live animals, firearms, crossbows, fireworks, medicines, cigarettes (although they seem to allow herbal cigarettes) etc. There are some oddities too, so it's worth checking the full list, not least because it's ever-changing:
www.amazon.co.uk/gp/help/customer/display.html/ref=hp_rel_topic?ie =UTF8&nodeId=201822800

FBA Packaging Restrictions
Most of these rules have been put in place to protect the product or the employees handling the product. For example, you have to ensure that sharp items (such as knives) have suitable packaging. The same goes for damage-prone items (such as china cups) and shock-sensitive items (such as certain types of hard drive). In addition, products sensitive to dust, dirt or humidity, have to be protected by transparent poly bags. (As an aside, Amazon does not accept pre-priced products, where the price is

printed on the product itself.) For further details, click here:
https://sellercentral.amazon.co.uk/gp/help/help.html?itemID=G200141500&language=en_GB

Hazmat products

Any product that is (or contains) a battery, liquid, powder or paste could be classified as a hazardous material (Hazmat). Depending on the ingredients or the packaging, products in different Amazon categories may be classified as Hazmat. Amazon has identified Hazmat products in the following categories: Automotive, Baby, Beauty and Personal Care, Consumer Electronics, Office, Pet Products, Sports and Outdoor, and Toys.

You need to be super-careful when dealing with such products. This is what Amazon says: "Even if a product is not currently rejected as Hazmat by our system, failure to comply with these policies may result in refusal of the inventory at the Amazon fulfilment centre, the disposal or return of inventory at your expense, the blocking of future shipments to the fulfilment centre, a charge for additional preparation or for non-compliance, the suspension of your selling privileges, or regulatory fines." In other words, breaching their Hazmat rules could be the end of your FBA business. I urge you to avoid such products, unless you're an experienced seller. For further details, click here:
https://sellercentral.amazon.co.uk/gp/help/help.html?itemID=G201003400&language=en_GB

Product safety

There are thousands of UK and EU documents covering product safety rules. As such, what I've written below is very much a summary.

Under the Sale of Goods Act 1979, all products must be "fit for purpose", be "of satisfactory quality" and "fit their description". Some products are covered by specific safety regulations and will need a CE mark. A CE mark is a manufacturer's guarantee that its product meets specified essential safety requirements set out in relevant European directives. Certain categories of products must bear CE marking if you intend to sell them in the EU:

- Toys.
- Electrical products.
- Construction products.
- Pressure vessels.
- Telecommunications equipment.
- Medical devices.
- Machinery, equipment and safety components.
- Personal protective equipment.
- Satellite station equipment.
- Gas appliances.
- Pressure equipment.
- Appliances (other than gas).
- Non-automatic weighing instruments and equipment.
- Measuring instruments.
- Recreational craft.
- Lift machinery.
- Equipment and protective systems for explosive atmospheres.
- In vitro diagnostic medical devices.
- Marine equipment.
- Safety components and subsystems for incorporation into cableway installations.
- Cableway equipment (ski tows etc.).

Where an item of equipment is covered by more than one directive, it must be CE marked under all applicable directives.

If you supply consumer products that aren't covered by these specific directives, they need not be CE marked. However, you still have a general duty to ensure they are safe for normal or reasonably foreseeable use under the General Product Safety Regulations 2005.

Click here for more details and useful links:
www.gov.uk/guidance/product-safety-for-manufacturers

To conclude

There has never been a better time to start a business. The knowledge of the world is at your fingertips – what you don't know you can find out. Creating your own brand and products is tremendously rewarding. Hopefully you'll make some money too. And there are countless people happy to help for free – you only have to glance at a few forums to see the giving nature of Amazon FBAers.

On that note, there are lots of Facebook groups dedicated to "Amazon.co.uk FBA". These three are very good:
- Amazon FBA UK.
- Amazon Wizards FBA Sellers Group
- Amazon UK FBA Sellers

Top tip: To find them you may need to narrow your search by country.

And don't give up. I read an extraordinarily droll blog written by an American FBA seller with a very British sense of humour ("Yet again I have failed," he wrote on a number of occasions.) However his eighth product was a big hit. He failed, dusted himself down, learned from his mistakes, bounced back and finally it came good. Nice work, fella!

Please review this book!

If you've enjoyed reading this book (or you didn't, but you learned lots), please leave a positive review. If you have spotted any mistakes or omissions, please email me: **nedbrowne@hotmail.com** so I can amend/improve future editions. Thank you!

Printed in Poland
by Amazon Fulfillment
Poland Sp. z o.o., Wrocław

58964197R00042